The French Quarter & Other

NEW ORLEANS SCENES

The French Quarter & Other

NEW ORLEANS SCENES

Written and Illustrated by
Joseph A. Arrigo

PELICAN PUBLISHING COMPANY
GRETNA 1984

First printing, June 1976
Second printing, March 1977
Third printing, August 1984

Library of Congress Cataloging in Publication Data

Arrigo, Joseph A., 1930—
    The French Quarter and other New Orleans scenes.

    Reprint. Originally published: New Orleans, 1976.
    1. Vieux Carré (New Orleans, La.)—Buildings—Guide-
books. 2. Architecture—Louisiana—New Orleans—Guide-
books. 3. Historic buildings—Louisiana—New Orleans—
Guide-books. 4. New Orleans (La.)—Buildings—Guide-
books. 5. New Orleans (la.)—Description—Guide-books.
I. Title.
F379.N56V527   1984   917.63'35   84.7670
ISBN 0-88289-455-2 (pbk.)

Manufactured in the United States of America

Published by Pelican Publishing Company, Inc.
1101 Monroe Street, Gretna, Louisiana 70053

CONTENTS

	Page
St. Louis Cathedral	13
The Cabildo	15
The Presbytere	17
Jackson Square	19
Pirates Alley	21
Cabildo Alley	23
Pere Antoine Alley at Royal Street	25
The Spanish Arsenal	27
The Upper Pontalba Building	29
The Lower Pontalba Building	31
Cafe Du Monde	33
The French Market	35
The Old United States Mint	37
Ursuline Convent	39
Beauregard House	41
Gallier House	43
Lafitte's Blacksmith Shop	45
Madame Johns's Legacy	47
Demarchy's Court	49
The Labranche Building	51
The Skyscraper Building	53
The Orleans Ballroom	55
Napoleon House	57
Court of the Three Arches' Slavequarters	59
Brulatour Courtyard	61
Antoine's Restaurant	63
Brennan's	65
The Louisiana Bank	67
The Louisiana Tourist Commission Building	69
Hermann/Grima House	71
The Fencing Master's Houses	73
The Old Absinthe House	75
Bourbon Street	77

The Olympia Brass Band ———————————————————————————————————— 79
Gallier Hall ——— 81
The St. Charles Streetcar ———————————————————————————————————— 83
The Louisiana Superdome ———————————————————————————————————— 85
Bueno Retiro ——— 87
The Delta Queen —— 89
The Natchez ——— 91
The Roman Candy Man ————————————————————————————————————— 93
Longue Vue House and Gardens ——————————————————————————————— 95

INTRODUCTION

New Orleans, well into its third century of existence, is one of the few American cities which retains and reflects both the old and the new in its lifestyle, attitude and architecture.

Its romantic history, authentic European architecture, fabulous restaurants and cuisine, music, exciting night life and entertainment, port and shipping activity, professional sports, large art colony, thoroughbred horse racing, boating, fishing, and world renowned festivals such as the Mardi Gras and the Spring Fiesta all combine to earn for New Orleans a reputation of being America's most interesting city.

New Orleans' unique and colorful history began in 1718 when the city was founded by Bienville as a French colony. It became an official colony of the French Crown in 1731 and was ceded to Spain by Louis XV in 1762. The Spanish ruled the city until 1803, in which year it was transferred back to France. In the same year — only a few months after its return to French rule — New Orleans and the vast Louisiana Territory (which now comprises all or part of 17 states) were sold to the United States by France for the sum of $15,000,000. The actual sales transaction of this famous "Louisiana Purchase" was completed in a room on the second floor of the Cabildo Building in the heart of the French Quarter.

The occurrence of many such events make the city a mecca for history buffs. A casual stroll through the French Quarter will provide anyone who has an interest in the past with enough material to digest for years.

Architecturally, the European flavor is probably best felt in the French Quarter. This area is also known as the *Vieux Carré* (Old Square). In the early years it was the entire city and to this day it remains a "city within a city." Today, there are only a few places left in the United States where a living, pulsating community such as the French Quarter remains basically the same as it was more than a hundred years ago. However, it shouldn't be surprising that New Orleans seems so European. Many of its attitudes, tastes and preferences were formed during its colonial period, which lasted more than a century.

The older buildings in the Quarter are constructed of a soft, locally made brick layed between cypress timbers and plastered over to prevent deterioration from the effects of the damp, semi-tropical climate. This type of construction is known as *briquette entre-poteaur* (brick between posts). Lafitte's blacksmith shop (shown on page 45) is an excellent example of this type of construction. Two great fires, in 1788 and 1794, destroyed much of the old city, which resulted in the local government requiring all new buildings to be constructed of brick and tile.

Though most of the Quarter is residential in character, there is much and varied commercial activity. At one time there were two major breweries operating within the Quarter boundaries; however, with the recent demise of the Jackson Brewing Company, this activity is no longer carried on. The elegant Royal Sonesta Hotel, completed in the early 1970's, occupies the site of the old Regal Brewery on Bourbon Street.

Most of the commercial activity is trade. A shopper's paradise, the French Quarter is one of the largest retail centers for antiques in the country. It also contains hundreds of quaint shops that sell wares for any and all interests.

Present also in the Quarter is one of the major art colonies of the United States. It is a place where art lovers can browse for hours in galleries, shops, alleys and the streets surrounding Jackson Square, viewing a variety of art of all schools in an atmosphere reminiscent of the Left Bank of Paris.

The city is a food lover's delight — gourmet restaurants abound, featuring French, Italian and Creole cooking which has become known all over the world. What is even more delightful for visitors to discover is a situation that is taken for granted by natives. Every section has many smaller restaurants and bistros that serve the same appetizing dishes as those with the great names.

The great interest in food is shared by Orleanians of all classes. Even harried businessmen usually find time for lingering two hour lunches and there's probably as much business transacted in New Orleans restaurants as in local office buildings.

Gumbo, po-boys, almost any type of fresh seafood, shrimp creole, crawfish bisque, crawfish etouffé, the best oysters found anywhere prepared in dozens of unique ways, boiled lake crabs, jambayla, pralines, red beans and rice, french market coffee and doughnuts, muffaletta sandwiches are some of the city's specialties that should be tasted by anyone who visits New Orleans.

New Orleans has the distinction of being the second largest port in the United States and the third largest in the world. Ships of all flags tie up or leave the Port of New Orleans at the rate of more than one each hour of each day. Value of the almost 20 million tons of cargo that is handled each year is over 8 billion dollars. Complete and well equipped facilities enable the Port of New Orleans to handle any and all types of cargo from grain to granite.

Music has been a most important part of the city's character since its beginning. New Orleans was the first city in America to establish an opera company on a permanent basis. Performances were as splendid as those in Europe, and at one time before the Civil War the city supported two complete French opera companies — and this at a time when the art form was struggling for acceptance in the city of New York. It is said that Creole audiences were most knowledgable and therefore most critical of the operatic renderings.

The most spectacular theatre where the opera companies performed was the French Opera House on Bourbon Street at Toulouse. This building was destroyed by fire in 1919. The French Opera House was designed by James Gallier. It was of Italian design, four stories high, and could seat more than 2000 for a performance. A large hotel now occupies its former site.

New Orleans is generally considered the birthplace of jazz, which first gained recognition as a new music form about the turn of the century. This traditional jazz music is now considered to be the first original art form to evolve from the new country. Some of the performers who were around at the creative beginnings of the most interesting music can still be heard at local jazz emporiums.

The traditional jazz marching bands are still very active, performing not only for the colorful jazz funerals to honor their peers, but also for almost any function where color and excitement is needed.

Two world famous New Orleans jazz musicians, Pete Fountain and Al Hirt, both operate their own clubs on Bourbon Street, where their versions of New Orleans Dixieland Jazz can be heard each night.

New Orleans is essentially a city for fun lovers. The wine flows freely 24 hours each day in many cafes and bistros. Some places closed only on election day and then quite reluctantly. It is said that New Orleans has more licensed liquor establishments per capita than any other large city in America.

Entertainment of just about any type is available for "day" or "night" people. The city has a fine symphony orchestra, operatic events on a regular basis, theatre, jazz emporiums, supper clubs, glittering night clubs, professional and amateur sports, thoroughbred horse racing at the nation's second oldest track, water sports and boating in adjacent Lake Pontchartrain, fishing and hunting nearby, amusement parks and just about every activity needed to make New Orleans a total "fun" city.

The Mardi Gras, however, is the essence of New Orleans to millions. The origins of this incomparable celebration go all the way back to pagan rites of spring; rites which evolved to the Christian observance of Fat Tuesday, the last day before lent.

It's almost impossible to define just what the Mardi Gras is. The best approach is to regard it as a magical state of mind which transforms all who participate in the celebration, either actively or as observers.

Mardi Gras is actually two celebrations. First, there's the celebration of the carnival organizations or "krewes" whose parades through the streets are usually followed by shining, formal balls complete with mock royalty, sumptuous tableaux and elegant processions for their invited guests and themselves.

Second, there's the "public" part of the celebration, consisting mostly of observing street parades complete with marching bands, flambeaux carriers, marching groups, horsemen, and gaudy floats, usually designed around some mythical theme. The floats carry masked and costumed riders, who are all members of the private "krewes," and who throw beads, trinkets and "doubloons" to the thousands who line the streets.

Mardi Gras day, Fat Tuesday, the final day of the celebration, is the day when just about everyone in the city forgets about work, dons a mask and costume, goes to see the seemingly endless parades, walks around, dances, sings, drinks and just has as much fun as possible until midnight, when the lenten season begins.

Other noteworthy annual events celebrated in New Orleans are the Jazz Festival, the Food Festival, several religious and ethnic festivals, and — second only to Mardi Gras — the Spring Fiesta. The Spring Fiesta is a several day long observance of the coming of Spring. It is celebrated mostly in the French Quarter with parades, patio tours, balcony singing, parties and a two day outdoor art show in Pirates Alley, featuring the work of hundreds of the city's artists.

In brief, New Orleans is one of the world's few truly unique cities; a great seaport, a cultural center, a fun-loving town that's just beginning to realize its potential as a business and industrial leader in the South. The people of New Orleans wouldn't trade their home for any place on earth. When you get right down to it, that says it all.

The French Quarter & Other
NEW ORLEANS
❧ SCENES ❧

ST. LOUIS CATHEDRAL

This church, named after the patron Saint of France, was built in 1794. It is the third such building on this site.

Don Andres Almonaster, wealthy Spanish nobleman and citizen of the new world city, furnished the funds and supervised construction of the new church which replaced the building lost in the great fire of 1788. The present "French" appearance of the church was accomplished in 1851 when the steeples were elevated and several other changes were made.

The Cathedral dominates the Jackson Square area and has become the symbol of New Orleans.

In recent years the Catholic church has elevated St. Louis Cathedral to the status of "Basilica"; it is the oldest cathedral/basilica still in use in the United States.

THE CABILDO

This building, which faces Jackson Square and stands alongside the St. Louis Cathedral, once housed the Spanish colonial government. The Cabildo was built in 1795 by Don Andres Almonaster Y Roxas. It was the site of the transfer in 1803 of Louisiana from Spain to France. The transfer of the vast Louisiana territory from France to the United States, historically known as the "Louisiana Purchase," also took place here in that same year.

The Cabildo is now one of the notable museums in the South.

THE PRESBYTERE

The Presbytere, at 751 Chartres Street, faces Jackson Square and flanks the St. Louis Cathedral on the northern side. Its construction was begun by Don Almonaster in the 1790's and was completed by the American government in 1813. The building was originally designed for use as a residence for the priests serving the Cathedral. The mansard roof was added at a later date to match that of the Cabildo.

The Presbytere is part of the Louisiana Museum complex and is open daily to the public. It contains many interesting topical displays.

JACKSON SQUARE

Jackson Square, originally called Place D'Arms, was laid out by Bienville, founder of the city, in 1720. It served as the public square and parade field in the city's early years and, for over 200 years, has been the site of many historical events.

The equestrian statue of Andrew Jackson in the center of the Square is the work of Clark Mills.

PIRATES ALLEY

Picturesque Pirates Alley, once known as Orleans Alley, runs along the south side of St. Louis Cathedral from Chartres St. through to Royal Street.

It is the site of an annual outdoor art show which is part of the New Orleans Spring Fiesta celebration.

CABILDO ALLEY

Cabildo Alley connects Pirates Alley with St. Peter Street. It is only one-half block long.

The building at the left of the illustration is unique in the French Quarter in that each floor has iron work of a different design.

PERE ANTOINE ALLEY
AT ROYAL STREET

Pere Antoine Alley lies between the St. Louis Cathedral and the Presbytere and runs from Chartres Street through to Royal Street.

The alley is named after Pere Antoine, the first rector of the St. Louis Cathedral.

St. Anthony's Garden at the rear of the Cathedral along Royal Street between Pere Antoine Alley and Pirates Alley was the site of many duels fought by young Creoles in the nineteenth century.

THE SPANISH ARSENAL

The Old Spanish Arsenal, at 615 St. Peter Street, stands at the rear of the Cabildo and is part of that museum complex. It was built to house the Spanish Arms (circa 1830) on the site of the Old Spanish Prison, which was erected in 1769.

THE UPPER PONTALBA BUILDING

The Upper Pontalba Building was one of two erected about 1850 by the Baroness De Pontalba, daughter of Don Andres Almonaster Y Roxas. It was designed by the famous architect of that time, James Gallier, Sr. It is said that the Pontalba buildings are the first such structures in America designed as apartment buildings.

This building is now owned by the city of New Orleans and is still used as residential apartments with shops on the lower floor.

THE LOWER PONTALBA BUILDING

The Lower Pontalba Buuilding is located across Jackson Square from its twin, the Upper Pontalba Building.

This building is owned by the Louisiana State Museum and houses the museum library and a museum exhibit which is a recreation of an 1850 apartment. There are many other shops along the first floor, but much of this structure is used as it was originally intended, as residential apartments.

The cast iron grill work on both Pontalba buildings was made in France and contains in its design the initials A P for the names of the Baroness Pontalba and her father Don Almonaster.

CAFE DU MONDE

Cafe du Monde, one of the world's famous coffee shops, is located at the extreme south end of the French Market complex. The shop never closes and serves traditional New Orleans "cafe au lait" (half chickory coffee, half boiled milk) and "beignets" (square French doughnuts).

The striped canopy shown in the illustration, a landmark for many years, was removed during the recent renovation and a beautiful fountain was installed in that area.

THE FRENCH MARKET

The original open-air market of Spanish and Colonial days, this site, according to local tradition, was first used by Indians as a bartering place.

The buildings were erected in stages — 1791, 1813, 1822 and 1872. The market was practically rebuilt as a Federal Work Progress Administration project during the 1930's depression years and has recently gone through another complete renovation process.

The French Market complex contains many types of shops and eating places. It also still functions as the market place for fresh fruit and produce grown on the many suburban "truck" farms.

THE UNITED STATES MINT

Located on Esplanade Avenue at the river, the old United States Mint, a huge structure more than 800 feet wide and 100 feet deep, stands on the site of Fort San Carlos, which protected the city in the beginning years and which was dismantled in 1821. The mint was built in 1835 by the United States Government. Millions of coins were minted there until the early 1920's when the government discontinued its operation.

The building has since been used as a Federal prison and a military center; but for several years has remained unoccupied. Title to the property was returned to the State of Louisiana in 1974 by the Federal Government, and a movement began to restore it to serve some functional use.

URSULINE CONVENT

The Ursuline Convent building, at 1114 Chartres Street, is supposedly the second oldest building in the Mississippi Valley. The structure was completed in 1734 for the Ursuline Order of Nuns, who had arrived in New Orleans in 1727. They were the first of their order to establish themselves in the new country.

The building has been occupied since its construction, and at one time the Louisiana Legislature used it as a meeting place.

A complete renovation of this beautiful building was completed in 1975.

BEAUREGARD HOUSE

Joseph Le Carpentier built Beauregard House in 1827 at 1113 Chartres Street, across from the Ursuline Convent. Mr. Le Carpentier was the grandfather of Paul Morphy, the world chess champion who was born in the house in 1837.

The famous Confederate General P.G.T. Beauregard lived in the house for a while after the Civil War, and the house has borne his name ever since.

Until her death in 1955, novelist Evelyn Keyes lived in Beauregard House and did much of her writing there. The house plays a prominent part in several of her novels.

Beauregard House is open daily to the public and contains many interesting artifacts and items collected by Miss Keyes from all over the world.

GALLIER HOUSE

Gallier House, at 1132 Royal Street, was erected by noted architect James Gallier, Jr., as a residence for his family.
The house and adjoining buildings have been beautifully restored in recent years. The entire complex is open to the public and contains all the furnishings that reflect the affluent lifestyle of the 1800's.

LAFITTE'S BLACKSMITH SHOP

On the corner of Bourbon and St. Phillip Street this old
cottage, built in the Creole style with brick between
posts *(briquetté entre poteaux)*, was supposedly
operated by Jean Lafitte and his brother as a blacksmith
shop which served as a "front" to cover their real
business of smuggling and piracy.

The "blacksmith shop" has been used as a bar for
many years.

MADAME JOHN'S LEGACY

This building bears the name of a fictional character in a story written by novelist George W. Cable.

Located at 632 Dumaine Street, Madame John's was built in 1788 on the site of a similar house destroyed in the great New Orleans fire. The original building was erected between 1722 and 1728, and shares with the Ursuline Convent the distinction of being one of the oldest structures in the Mississippi Valley still in existence.

Madame John's legacy is part of the Louisiana State Museum complex. The main building and the slave quarters at the rear of the property have been recently restored as a permanent museum exhibit.

DEMARCHY'S COURT
AND STAIRWAY

The beautiful courtyard and curved stairway at 625 Toulouse Street has been admired by local artists and tourists for years.

The building which contains this courtyard and stairway was built in 1807 by Jean Antoine Demarchy, a well known builder of the early 1800's.

THE LABRANCHE BUILDING

This building, at 700 Royal Street, was erected in the 1830's for Jean Baptiste Labranche. It is directly across from the "Skyscraper" building on the corner of St. Peter Street.

Msr. Labranche's house is one of the most photographed in the French Quarter because of the striking cast iron balcony railings, whose design incorporates beautifully symmetrical oak leaves and acorns.

THE SKYSCRAPER BUILDING

The "Skyscraper" building at the corner of Royal and St. Peter streets acquired its unusual name because it was the first four story building in the French Quarter.

This structure has also been called "Sieur George's House" after a fictional character who lived here in one of George W. Cable's stories.

It was built by Dr. Yves Le Mounier, a New Orleans physician, about 1811. His initials can still be seen in the balcony railings.

THE ORLEANS BALLROOM

During the golden years before the Civil War, the Orleans Ballroom, at 717 Orleans Street, was the scene of the popular quadroon balls where white Creole gentlemen danced with the legendary beautiful young girls of some Negro blood.

The building was at one time used by the Louisiana Legislature as its meeting place. In 1881 it was purchased by a wealthy Black man and turned over to the Sisters of the Holy Family, an order of Black nuns.

In recent years the ballroom has become part of a large hotel which occupies most of the square.

NAPOLEON HOUSE

Located at 500 Chartres Street, Napoleon House was originally the residence of Nicholas Girod, Mayor of New Orleans.

Legend has it that Mayor Girod offered the home to former Emperor Napoleon if he could escape his exile from the Island of St. Helena, however the records show that the building was not actually erected until many months after Napoleon's death.

SLAVE QUARTERS AT THE COURT OF THREE ARCHES

Located at 633 Toulouse Street, this structure was built by Dr. Germain Ducatel in 1825.

It is an interesting note that railings of cypress were used on the balconies rather than the usual cast or wrought iron. An art gallery has occupied the lower floor of this building for years.

BRULATOUR COURTYARD

The building which this courtyard serves was built in 1816 by Francis Seignouret, a New Orleans wine dealer and cabinet-maker. The property was acquired by Ernest Brulatour in 1870, and this most famous of the French Quarter courtyards has carried his name ever since.

Television station WDSU-TV has occupied the property since it began broadcasting in 1948.

Brulatour Courtyard is at 520 Royal Street.

ANTOINE'S RESTAURANT

At 713 St. Louis Street, this world famous restaurant has been in continuous operation for more than a century.

Oysters Rockefeller, probably its most famous dish, was invented here for a visit by the famous financier.

The decor is sparse; but the New Orleans dishes and a remarkable wine list make Antoine's a must for everyone whose interests are culinary.

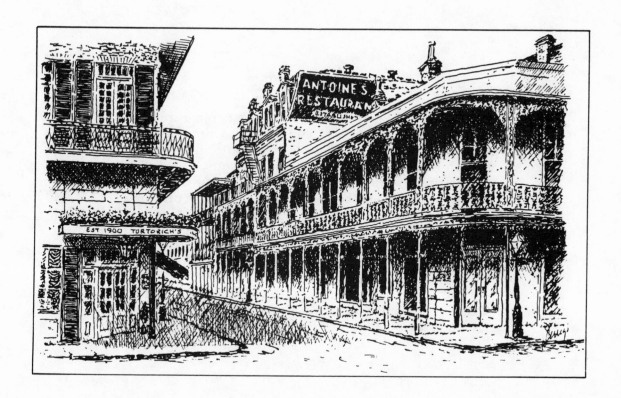

BRENNAN'S

Located at 417 Royal Street, this famous restaurant,
noted for its fantastic Creole breakfasts, occupies a
building built circa 1796 for the great-grandfather of
French impressionist painter Edgar Degas.

During the course of its history, this building has
served as the site of the Louisiana Bank and at one time
was the home of world chess champion Paul Morphy,
who died in a second floor bathroom.

In 1975, Brennan's Restaurant was partially
destroyed by fire, but since has been beautifully
restored.

Almost every noted personality who visits New
Orleans dines at Brennan's. Its reservation lists have
tables reserved sometimes 10 years in advance.

THE LOUISIANA BANK

This building, at 401 Royal Street, was built in 1831 to house the Louisiana State Bank. The initials L.S.B. can still be seen in the center of the second floor balcony railing.

Benjamin Latrobe, who designed a wing of the Nation's Capitol Building in Washington, D.C., also was the designer of this building, but died of yellow fever before it was completed.

The Louisiana Bank Building contains a very interesting domed ceiling on the lower level. For many years the building has housed an antique shop.

THE LOUISIANA TOURIST
COMMISSION BUILDING

Located at 334 Royal Street, this building is one of
several that was used by the Bank of Louisiana. It was
constructed circa 1826 primarily for use by the bank.
James Gallier designed the iron fence and the Royal
Street entranceway, both of which were added in the
1840's.

The structure is architecturally one of the finest
along Royal Street. It was used by the American Legion
for years, and has recently been restored by the Greater
New Orleans Tourist and Convention Commission. It is
open daily to visitors who are graciously received with
free New Orleans-style coffee and tourist information.

HERMANN-GRIMA HOUSE

This house, at 820 St. Louis St., was built in 1831 as a residence for the family of Samuel Hermann. It was sold to a prominent notary, Felix Grima, in 1844 and remained in possession of the Grima family until 1924, when it was acquired by the Christian Women's Exchange.

The Hermann-Grima House is now listed in the National Register of Historic Places. The entire complex of house, garconiere, kitchen, stable and courtyards is open to the public. It is probably the most complete representation of affluent ante-bellum Creole home life in the French Quarter.

Hermann-Grima House served as officers quarters for the Army of the North during the Civil War occupation of New Orleans.

THE FENCING MASTERS HOUSES

The four-story structures at the corner of Exchange Alley and Conti Street once housed the Academies of the Fencing Masters. During the "golden" era before the Civil War, these fencing schools were attended by almost all of the gentlemen of the city.

THE OLD ABSINTHE HOUSE

The Old Absinthe House, at the corner of Bourbon Street and Bienville Street, was built about 1806 as a shop and residence for Pedro Font and Francisco Juncadella, who were prominent food and liquor importers.

The building's name came from a potent, licorice-flavored liquor called Absinthe, which was served to Creole gentlemen and businessmen in this tavern. The Old Absinthe House is still one of the most popular bars in the French Quarter, where the custom is to attach one's business or calling card to the wall.

Legend has it that Andrew Jackson and Jean Lafitte planned the defense of New Orleans from the British in the War of 1812 in a secret chamber on the second floor of the Old Absinthe House. Several other places in the French Quarter have had this same legendary claim made about them.

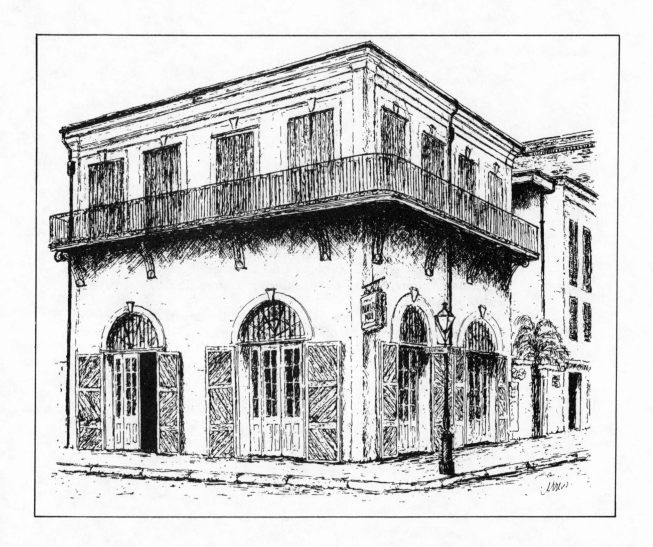

BOURBON STREET

Named for the French Royal Family, Bourbon Street is the street of honky tonks, stripteasers, jazz and, in more recent years, massage parlors, rock joints and almost everything else. The beautiful Royal Sonesta occupies one side of the entire 300 block and several of New Orleans' famous eating establishments have Bourbon Street addresses.

New Orleans jazz greats Pete Fountain and Al Hirt both operate their clubs on Bourbon Street.

It would be hard to imagine anyone visiting New Orleans without taking at least a casual stroll along this most remarkable street.

THE OLYMPIA BRASS BAND

The Olympia Brass Band, shown here being inimatably led by its Grand Marshall, the late "Fats" Houston, is one of several marching jazz bands active in the city.

The jazz parade is still quite a common occurrence in New Orleans and, whether the marching jazz band is playing for the funeral of a fellow jazzman or for a less somber event, it is usually seen with a "second line" of jazz enthusiasts tagging behind.

GALLIER HALL

Gallier Hall is located at 545 St. Charles Street, across from Lafayette Square. It was designed and built by James Gallier, Sr., in 1850, and was used as City Hall until 1957.

The building is a beautiful and lasting example of the Greek revival architecture which was so popular in the middle 1800's. Its intricately carved pediment shows figures which represent justice, liberty and commerce.

ST. CHARLES STREETCAR

St. Charles Ave. is one of New Orleans' most beautiful streets, extending from Canal Street through the famous garden district, and is lined with some of the South's most elegant and distinguished homes.

The St. Charles streetcar, which runs along this beautiful and interesting route, is the last in the city and one of the few remaining electric trolley lines still operating in the United States.

THE LOUISIANA SUPERDOME

The Louisiana Superdome, located in the heart of the city across from the City Hall, is one of the largest buildings of its kind in the world. The 161 million dollar stadium arches to a height of 273 feet, covers 52 acres of land, and has a flexible seating arrangement that can be adjusted for events that require anywhere from 10,000 to 95,000 seats.

It is the home of the New Orleans Saints professional football team and the New Orleans Jazz basketball team.

BUENO RETIRO

This small plantation house is located below the city of New Orleans on the site of the battle of New Orleans, which took place in 1812.

The house was built in 1840 from designs of James Gallier, Sr. Judge Rene Beauregard, son of the famous Confederate General P.G.T. Beauregard, acquired the house shortly after the Civil War.

It is sometimes called Beauregard House and is open to the public as a museum honoring the battle which took place on its grounds. The building also serves as an office for the United States Park Service, which maintains the park.

THE DELTA QUEEN

The Delta Queen is an antique sternwheeled steamboat that is listed in the National Register of Historic Places.

Because the vessel's structure is made largely of wood, a special act of Congress was passed exempting it from certain provisions of the Safety at Sea Law of 1966. This special exemption allows the Delta Queen to operate as an active passenger carrying vessel until November 1, 1978.

The Delta Queen features a variety of cruises on the Mississippi and Ohio Rivers between New Orleans and Cinncinnati.

NATCHEZ IX

The Natchez IX is a 1600 passenger, steel hulled prototype of an old fashioned stern wheel steamboat.

On July 4, 1975, a tradition was renewed when the Natchez IX raced the "Delta Queen," the veteran Mississippi steamboat. The Natchez IX was victorious, as was one of its predecessors, the Natchez VI, which also won its famous race with the steamboat "Robert E. Lee" in the 19th century.

The race is scheduled to be an annual event.

THE ROMAN CANDY MAN

A familiar sight in Uptown New Orleans is the Roman
Candy Man, one of the city's last peddling wagon
vendors. Sam Cortese, who died in 1969, began selling
the Italian taffy candy in 1910 out of his coal wagon.
He had the candy wagon built by a New Orleans
wheelright in 1915. It is still in use by his grandson,
Ronnie Kottemann, who sells the same traditional
candy made from his great-grandmother's recipe.

LONGUE VUE HOUSE
AND GARDENS

Longue Vue, an eight-acre urban estate, was the home of New Orleans philanthropists Edgar and Edith Stern. The mansion, built in 1942, echoes the Greek Revival architectural style. The interior was designed for comfortable living and elegant entertaining.

Formal gardens surround the house, the largest being the Spanish court, simulating the Generalife Garden of the Alhambra in Grenada, Spain. Fountains, mosaic walks, and original sculpture contribute to the Moorish splendor of this estate.

Longue Vue is one of America's most beautiful estates. It is open year round to visitors.

Longue Vue House & Gardens, New Orleans

95